THE

SUCCESS

Tiny Changes big Results

THE SUCCESS

How to find and increase your motivation

IMPRINT

Text and Content

@ COPYRIGHT 2024

BY MARIA VALLEETSY

C/O IMPRESSUM-SERVICE VALLEETSY

PADRE BURGOS AVE,

1000 METRO MANILA

THE SUCCESS

Introduction

Who doesn't want to be more motivated in life so we can accomplish everything that we want while still having the fire burning inside of us? This is usually easier said than done.

Finding your motivation is sometimes like trying to find an elusive unicorn, one that everyone is trying to get a hold of and only a few of the fortunate ones are able to accomplish this. However, this doesn't have to be the case.

Motivation is like a muscle, and it can be cultivated and pushed to grow and become much stronger with just a few simple applications and a few minor changes in your life.

With the right positive changes in your lifestyle, you will benefit on many different levels, including psychological and physical, along with other areas of your life.

Just by making better choices for yourself, you are going to reap the benefits. This isn't going to be easy. In fact, it is going to take hard work, and you will need to know what it is you're doing.

By the end of this book, you will have a clear road full of obvious choices that you will be able to take for yourself when it comes to being the motivated and motivating person that you want to be.

Whether you are trying to get the most out of your time, inspire those around you, or lead your company to success, these tips will give you the motivation you need to succeed.

Chapter 1
What is Motivation?

Motivation is the force that guides you to do what you do. It is the reason behind all of your actions. What you think, do, say, and act on is all inspired and originated from somewhere. Have you ever taken the time to ponder over the source of all that you do?

It isn't just the actions, but also the repetitions of your actions that are driven by motivation.

When you are motivated enough, you are able to accomplish your goals and achieve everything you've set out to do.

The word motivation is a derivative of the word 'motive.' Motive can best be described as the real reason behind everyone's actions. It shouldn't be confused with its cousin 'intention,' which is an entirely different concept. Here is an example to help you understand the differences between motive and intention.

Justin, who is in his thirties, and who has two kids to feed and a household to manage finds himself unemployed. Desperate, he turns to stealing from others. One day he crosses paths with a wealthy businessperson who is holding a large amount of money in this wallet.

Seeing his chance, Justin takes out a knife and darts toward the man.

In the above situation, Justin intends to point a knife at the wealthy businessman and steal his money.

However, Justin's motivation is to feed his starving children. Motivation is a bigger set than intention. It is the real reason behind all of our actions.

Therefore, in the above example, motivation can be roughly defined as the actual reason or push that made Justin take action and think what he thinks. We can conclude that motivation is a large version of intention that goes beyond our immediate wants or desires.

The origin of motivation has two theories, the Natural vs. Rational theory and the Content vs. Process theory.

Let's take some time to explore both to get a better understanding of what each says on the matter.

Natural vs. Rtional Theories

Nature has given man excellent survival instincts. Because of this, whatever actions we take, whether consciously or otherwise, are ultimately aimed at helping us to survive, or also known as 'making the evolutionary cut.'

On the other hand, through observation, skills, and experience, we have achieved the power of rational thinking and being able to make good decisions. These powers of the mind are not distributed equally among the population. Not everyone has the same footing when it comes to possessing rational-centric powers.

Advocates of each theory argue that it is their claim that wins over the other. Nature, while providing us with our survival instincts extended its application to getting motivated. One's motivations are derived from one's instinct to survive.

On the other hand, the rational theory advocates claim that everyone has their own set of skills depending on how much they have worked toward it. Motivation in such a scenario is derived from one's experiences and talents.

Content vs. Process Theories

The second theory is Content vs. Process. It is of the idea that anything that you see is the result of an input that has been converted into the required output through a set of procedures.

There is a definite process involved in coming into existence of anything that is an outcome of any kind. Motivation, when viewed through the prism of process theory, requires merely that there need to be specific conditions for it to be manufactured.

On the other hand, the content theory argues that the conditions for the successful manufacturing of human motivations depends on the situation and can vary from situation to situation.

It isn't necessary that the kind and amount of motivation that James generates or receives is the same kind and amount of motivation that is generated or received by Stephanie. They vary because of their source and the situations that are dictated at their birth, rather than their destination.

Source of Motivation

The truth about motivation is that it requires more than just saying to yourself that you want to make more money or that you want to get a task done so that you don't have to do it anymore. This isn't motivation, but instead, they are the reasons for having to do something or an effect of having accomplished your goal. You can't build your motivation from these.

You need a purpose of a cause to rally behind to draw your real inspiration. You need it to be the fire that ignites you and gives you the passion that you need to move forward, even in the face of challenges. Here are some of the most useful sources for improving your motivation.

Family

Having a sense of family can be a source of intense motivation and is one that has taken root within our lives for centuries. The sense of honor and duty that you have to your family can lead you to achieve success in the goals that you have set out to accomplish. This sense of family is something that many people take to mean something tangible beyond anything else that could inspire them.

The desire to leave a legacy that transcends yourself and that you can pass on to future generations is a strong motivating factor for many. A family is the kind of motivation that led to the building of empires and to the construction of large buildings and enterprises that have lived on long after the founders were gone. If you have a family that you love intensely, then this is a source of motivation that you might be seeking.

Glory

Gaining glory is a profoundly personal desire that encompasses a lot of motivational sources that are within people. Perhaps you need to accomplish things in order to find validation that is lasting and powerful.

If you are the kind of person that seeks praise and power for the accomplishments you've achieved, then glory might be an extremely powerful motivating factor for you.

The heroes and warriors of old used to accomplish great things all in the name of glory. While wealth leads to pleasure and comfort, it is also something that fades. Glory, something that reflects back on you, is going to fill you with the sense of power and accomplishment that you crave.

It is a personal motive and its drive to make your mark upon the world. If you are someone that wants your name to go down in history, then glory will be your motivator and the push you need to accomplish your goals.

The Cause

When it comes to making your mark upon the world, you aren't as interested in it being your name, but rather the name of the cause. Whether it's service to a nation, religion, or the ability to give back to the people of the world, that is your cause. Your cause is what you want to see elevated to glory, and it is something that you should embrace as a source of strength and power within your life.

You are a vital part of your cause, and only you can provide it with the strength and expansion that's required to make it something that is truly beautiful, enduring, and powerful. Whatever your cause, make sure that you do it justice and that you continuously draw strength from it, and that it is your guiding light through the darkness.

Once you've discovered your source of motivation, you need to figure out how to hold on to it. You need to find ways to avoid burning out so that you can keep your motivation strong and find success.

Chapter 2 – Developing Healthy Morning Habits

One of the best ways to start your day

off with enough motivation to

accomplish your daily goals is to

develop healthy morning habits and start your day off on a positive note. When you can train yourself to develop healthy habits, you will find that your energy levels through the day have increased dramatically.

This will result in getting the extra boost you need to make you feel that you are ready to take on your day. You want to be pumped and ready to go, so that you can focus on the tasks that you need to accomplish that day.

Setting small goals for yourself is an integral part of directing you toward your long-term goals. Your morning ritual is a critical factor in being able to accomplish your goals no matter how large or small. Starting your day with a positive ritual will help to revitalize you. If you can, you want to try to teach yourself how to stay focused on a single task. Focusing on a single task at the time will help you to reach your broader goals.

Creating a daily morning ritual will have you jumping out of your bed to greet the new day rather than dragging yourself out of bed feeling tired and glum before your day even has the chance to get started.

You may be like many people and believe that you just can't do anymore in the morning because you are already struggling to get through your morning as it is. You may not see yourself as a morning person. Even if you have your doubts about creating a morning ritual, you will gain the tools that you need to make the changes in your life and increase your motivation.

Adding the following routine to your morning ritual will provide you with numerous benefits. The first 30 minutes of the routine will give you the energy you need to get up and, and it will help you to stay energized throughout your day.

If you can commit to devoting your early mornings to work on selfimprovement, you will be much less likely to skip the routing and by working on your self-improvement in the mornings the rest of your day will be more productive.

Becoming active in the early morning can be an incredibly daunting prospect. However, with some practice and patience, you will adjust. The great thing is that you will be in control of when your day begins. You will realize that the benefits that you are getting from this change in your life are well worth going through the initial aches and pains of change.

Rather than continuing to do your daily unproductive morning routine, learn how to get your tasks done in order of priority by setting up a daily planner for yourself. Replace the pointless actions that you've been doing every morning with ones that are going to add real meaning to your life. Finding an energized ritual is going to help to boost your energy levels and increase your motivation throughout your day.

Gain More Exposure to Natural Light

The first thing that you should do in the morning is open your blinds and curtains to allow more natural light to flow into your room. Your body is programmed to wake up to natural light. If it is during the winter and it's dark in the mornings where you live, then you may need to get up and turn on the lights.

There are special lights that you can buy, called "happy light" that simulates natural light. So, while you are doing other things, like gathering your clothing, keep exposing yourself to the natural light. There are also several kinds of alarm clocks on the market today that will simulate the rising sun in your bedroom.

Washing Up Ritual

When we take the time to wash in the morning, this helps our brain realize that the day has begun. To get the most out of the washing up ritual, try to incorporate these steps into your new daily morning routine. When you first wake up:

1. Wash your face with hot water and a facial cleanser.

2. Finish up with a splash of cold water.

3. Take a short shower. Don't worry about washing your hair or using soap, just get your body wet.

4. Dry off and get dressed in fresh clothes.

5. Brush your teeth and rinse with mouthwash.

Following these simple steps, every morning will signal to your brain that it is time to start your day.

Get Hydrated

After you've finished your washing up ritual, you need to make sure that you get yourself hydrated by drinking at least one, eightounce glass of water. If you enjoy a strong cup of coffee in the morning, that's fine, just make sure you also drink a bottle of water with it, so you don't become dehydrated.

Feed Your Body and Mind

We all know that breakfast is the most important meal of the day. However, you want to try to avoid overeating in the morning because this will only make you feel sluggish and slow you down for the rest of the day. It's best if you eat a small serving of an antioxidant smoothie, or an egg on a muffin, or a small bowl of berries or a piece of fruit, or even some yogurt with nuts sprinkled on top.

Get Your Body Moving

If you want to stay motivated throughout your day, then you need to get your brain running effectively. In order to do this, you need to get your heart pumping. To get your heart pumping first thing in the morning, try one of the following quick exercises:

- 25 jumping jacks
- 25 wall push-ups

- 25 lunges
- 25 crunches
- Three yoga poses
- Quick 10-minute walk or jog

To help get your senses charged up in the morning, you can try dabbing a bit of peppermint oil under your nose or brush your teeth with mint toothpaste. Mint has been proven to help with increasing mental awareness. You can also try listening to a particular song every morning that you know gets your blood pumping to the point that you are ready to do some dancing.

Make a Connection with Your Passion

Every morning, choose to participate in an activity that will energize you are you ready yourself for your hour of selfimprovement. You can use the energized activity as a bridge to your hour-long activity.

As you finish the energizing segment of your new daily morning routine, include something that will make you want to take action like meditating about your goal for a few minutes, reading a blog that focuses on your interest, or keep a journal of your progress. You want to make sure that this activity can be completed in under 30 minutes.

What Not to Do in Your Morning Ritual

Some habits can quickly kill your energy and motivation, so it is best that you avoid doing things like looking at social media sites first thing in the morning, watching TV, surfing the internet, interacting with others, and wasting your time with morning gossip.

You need to avoid doing these kinds of activities in the morning because they will slow you down and kill your motivation. It is best to leave these activities for later in the day.

In the first 30 minutes of your day, you want to try to make everything as easy as possible for you to accomplish the goals you've set for yourself. If you find it difficult to turn your daily routine into a habit, keep working on it and making any necessary adjustments that you may need to ensure that you include everything you need in the morning.

Chapter 3 – Focusing on Self-Improvement

Once you've gotten to the point where you have your energizing routine down, the next step that you will want to take is planning out your hour of self-improvement.

You should try to commit to at least one hour every morning to work on your self-improvement, however, if this won't work with your schedule, then you should aim for 30 minutes. You can begin with a 30 window, but you might eventually find that you can increase this time to a solid hour.

The main thing that you want to focus on is that you are setting aside time in your morning to dedicate to completing a lifechanging activity that will increase your motivation for success. Many people find that they are able to stay focused on their lifechanging activities for 45 to 60 minutes, but find that their motivation and focus drop after an hour.

Focus is an essential aspect of this commitment. There are too many of us that spend too much time multitasking, and not spending our time just focusing on a single task at a time. It has been shown in several studies that we are actually more efficient when we tackle one thing at a time.

They also show that we tend to learn better when we are focused exclusively on one thing at a time. Focus is indeed essential when you are trying to change your habits and improve your life.

This step in the process will require you to choose an activity for your self-improvement time that will have an impact in reaching your goals. Some people will try to take on two goals at the same time, like losing weight and taking cooking classes. However, as stated before, trying to work on two targets at a time won't work.

You need to focus on just one of your goals at a time, at least until you get to the point where you feel comfortable taking on another target. For example, perhaps you can start by taking a cooking class that will teach you how to prepare healthy meals properly.

Once you have the knowledge on how to cook healthy meals, then you can start to tackle your other goal of losing weight. Knowing the right foods to prepare will make dieting that much easier for you to tackle. You will be more successful if you can commit to choosing one goal at a time to tackle.

If your goal is to lose weight, you can keep yourself more motivated by designing a weekly meal planner and tracking your food intake daily. Keep track of your weight loss by weighing yourself daily and keeping careful track of everything you eat throughout the day.

Planning Your Goals for Each Morning

The reason why you should set aside the self-improvement time in the morning is to help you improve your life in the here and now. The energizing portion of your morning routine will more than likely stay the same; however, your self-improvement time will change as you accomplish your goals.

For example, you have decided that you want to dedicate your self-improvement time to going on a power walk every morning to help improve your physical fitness. Eventually, power walking won't be enough to challenge you early in the day.

This might lead you to replace it with jogging at a faster pace, or maybe even a career goal. Here are some activities that you might be interested in doing during your morning selfimprovement time.

Start an Online Business

You might be interested in starting an online business or writing a book, or even interested in getting into affiliate marketing. You can use your morning self-improvement time to focus on the steps you need to take to get your online business started.

Maybe you need to research the different companies that offer affiliate marketing opportunities, or you can start spending your hour outlining the chapters of a book you've always wanted to write.

Or maybe you can spend your hour creating networking relationships with other marketers. Use your self-improvement time to work on whatever it is you need to start your online business.

Lose Weight

Does your current weight have an adverse effect on your life? For most people, when they lose weight, they find that they gain a number of benefits on multiple levels from losing just a few pounds.

If you decide to spend your self-improvement time concentrating on losing weight you might want to consider checking in with a friend when you check your weight. This will help to hold you accountable in making sure to follow up.

If weight loss is your goal, then you want to make sure that you pack a healthy lunch every day so that you aren't tempted to grab fast food on your lunch break. You also need to choose a form of exercise that will provide you with the cardio workout that you need daily.

You can choose to participate in an activity like biking, swimming, power-walking, or running. You should also try to make a schedule for yourself where you are doing different kinds of exercises throughout the week rather than doing the same activities every day.

Learn Something New

You may want to utilize your hour of self-improvement time participating in activities that you will enjoy while learning something new. Perhaps you have an interest in learning how to paint using watercolors.

You can use your self-improvement time to learn the various techniques needed to create watercolor paintings. You'll spend this time improving your art skills. You can take a course for beginners in drawing or read a book that will walk you through the process and necessary steps to help you get started.

Whatever it is that you want to learn about, spend your morning self-improvement time working toward your goal of learning something new. There are plenty of resources online, for anything your mind can dream up.

Increase Your Spirituality

You may be at a time in your life where you feel that you are in need of some improvement in your mindfulness and spirituality.

You can increase your spirituality in a number of ways, but here are a few suggestions on how you can spend your morning selfimprovement hour.

- Read spiritual texts and take notes on what inspired you.
- Spend time meditating or praying.
- Practice mindfulness techniques by observing your own breathing and tuning into the quiet sounds of the early morning.
- Write down ten blessings.
- Walk around in an area where you gain inspiration.

- Write down ways that you can give back or participate in charity projects and organizations.
- Take action on your list of ways to give back and do it within the next 24 hours.

- Learn to extend kindness to those that have disappointed or hurt you in your life.
- Write a letter to yourself, telling yourself how your spiritual growth has had an impact on your friends and family.
- Include daily activities in your life that will feed your soul.

Increase Your Physical Activity

You may want to think about joining a workout class if your goal is
to increase your physical activity. If you are overweight or haven't done a lot of physical activity lately, you may want to

start with an activity that is done in the water.

Working out in the water is a healthy and safe way to increase your physical activity. You may also want to head outside and take a brisk walk or hike. There are many activities that you can do to reach your goal of increasing your physical activity levels.

Build Up Your Confidence

A huge motivation killer is a lack of confidence. If you want to increase your motivation, then you will have to work on your selfconfidence. Here are some activities that can help you build up your self-confidence and increase your motivation.

- Visualize yourself succeeding in a particular scenario, creating a movie with you as the main character or star of the show. Go through something that usually intimidates you, step-by-step with you accomplishing what you set out to do in your visualization.

This is a common practice among professional athletes. Studies have proven that using visualization techniques can increase success rates even more than actual practice, even for physical activities. Build up your confidence by visualizing your success for at least ten minutes every day.

- Use a journal to write down three specific things that you did the day before that made you like yourself. These can be simple things, but it is essential that they are precise and truthful.

- Learn how to assert yourself confidently and clearly. Think of difficult situations that you may find yourself in, then create two-line scripts for these difficult situations. If you have someone in your life that is always talking down to you and making you feel horrible, take the time to write down what you can say to them to stop them from talking to you in such a negative manner.

Practice with yourself by speaking the script out loud while you look in the mirror. Observe your posture and make sure to stand up straight and with confidence.

- Take the time to make sure that you look presentable. Make sure that you wear clean clothes and that you are properly groomed. Once you have cleaned yourself up, look at yourself in the mirror and think of the three favorite things about your appearance that you like.
This positive thinking will help to build your confidence.

All of these self-improvement activities will help you become more excited about your days and increase your motivation.

Remember, completing your hour of self-improvement time in the morning will allow you to carry that energy and motivation throughout the rest of your day.

Chapter 4 – Trading Bad Habits for Good Ones

Most of us have a terrible habit or three that we would like to change or trade in for a good habit. Instead of procrastinating with your long list of never ending excuses as to why you can't trade in your bad habits, perhaps it may be time to make the trade.

If you want to increase your energy levels and motivation, then having some good practices are sure to help you improve your motivation so you can finally achieve your goals.

For the majority of us, change isn't easy because we tend to be creatures of habit, even if those habits aren't so great. An excellent way to approach making the necessary changes in your lifestyle is to give yourself a firm start date. When you can give yourself a firm start date, it allows you the time you need to adjust and ready yourself for the upcoming change.

With a firm start date, you can get the preparations done that will help to make the transition from your bad habits to some good habits much easier to do. For example, if you want to give up smoking, it is much easier to accomplish if you replace the habit with a good one.

You might want to consider trading your lousy habit in for some regular physical activity. If you feel that you are spending too much time on the couch channel surfing, you might want to choose an activity that will get you up and moving for at least 30 minutes a day.

Or you may decide to start reading for 30 minutes a day rather than playing video games. If you are trying to lose weight, you can work on replacing one high calorie, high fat snack with a healthier choice, along with adding more physical activity.

Swapping out bad habits with physical activities is excellent because not only are you getting rid of your bad habits, but you are also committing to living a healthier life. Here are some different physical exercises that you can start to incorporate into your life to begin to eliminate your bad habits.

Once you've chosen a particular activity that you want to replace your bad habit with, you will want to put a start date on your calendar. By setting a start date, and writing it down, it will make the transition more real to you, which will make you more likely to stay committed to replacing your bad habits.

You also want to be sure to pick an activity that you will enjoy because you will be more likely to stay motivated to keep doing it on a regular basis. With regular daily physical activities, you will find that your energy levels will start to increase and you will have more motivation to reach your goals.

Walking

Walking is an excellent form of physical activity, especially if you have been inactive for a while. If you have a dog or child, they will be more than happy to escort you on your walks. Having a walking partner is a great way to motivate and encourage you to get up and go for a walk every day.

Once you get used to walking, you can build it up in pace to make it more challenging. Either way, you will gain the energy boost you need to accomplish your goals and become successful.

Swimming

This can be a fun way to get some exercise. There are water exercise classes that are available at most public pools. You could join a class, and on the days that you don't have a class, you can participate in another kind of activity, like walking.

It is always a good idea to mix a few physical activities up throughout the week to prevent you from getting bored with the same old routine. It is also a good idea to change things up when you feel that you are losing interest.

Running

Once you've become used to completing the more straightforward basic exercises, you may want to start incorporating running a few times a week. You have to walk before you run, especially when you are building an activity routine that will suit your level of fitness. You don't want to create goals that are out of your reach.

Feeling overwhelmed can make you feel unmotivated and will kill your motivation. You want to make sure that your physical goals are within reach so that you can be sure that you are exercising at a safe level. You definitely don't overdo it because it can lead to doing more damage than good.

Yoga

Practicing yoga is a healthy way for you to get physical exercise, as well as improving your mindfulness. It is an exercise that you can choose to do at home, or you can join a local class with a friend. Joining a class with a friend will help to keep you motivated to continue your yoga practice.

Meditation

Regular meditation practice is an excellent form of exercise to give both your body and mind a positive energy boost. There are different kinds and levels of reflection that you can start. As with yoga, this activity is something that you can do either at home or in a group or class setting.

Bike Riding

Take a bike ride is another fun way that you can incorporate some exercise into your daily routine. It is something that you can do by yourself or with your family. Heading out with your loved ones is one way to make exercising fun.

Dance Classes

Joining a dance class is another fun and exciting way to get some exercise and replace your bad habits. Not only will you increase your physical activity, but it will get you out of your house and socializing and will provide you with a significant energy boost.

Replacing your bad habits with physical exercise is not only good for you but when you are in good physical health, you will have an endless supply of motivation. Living a healthy lifestyle can also help you to reach your goals faster by providing you with the energy you need to accomplish everything that you've set out to do.

Chapter 5 – Decrease Stress and Increase Energy

You may not know this, but stress is actually a chemical reaction, a hormonal chemical reaction, that occurs in your body because of a perceived threat. During a threatening situation, hormone cortisol appears in your blood, causing your heartbeat to increase.

Stress at one time was humanity's lifesaver.

However, the link that stress has to motivation is incredibly complex. For example, when motivation kicks in so that you can finish your project by its deadline, one will naturally feel a bit stressed.

The level of stress that you feel in this situation should be subtle, just enough to get your heart pumping more quickly to your brain. This is commonly referred to as the fight-or-flight response. This survival response that is linked to better performance.

However, if you are getting too much stress, it can be incredibly unproductive regarding you being motivated. Chronic stress causes many diseases and conditions. It can lead to an unhappy and cumbersome life. If you are unhappy and ill, then you aren't going to have the motivation to move forward in your life.

There is a myriad of things that can cause stress in your life. What one person might stress about another may shrug it off.
Regardless of the source of the stress, it affects everyone on both a physical and emotional level.

If you suffer from chronic stress, then it is likely that you become easily agitated and frustrated when things don't go your way. This can have lasting effects on your relationships, your eating habits, your motivation, and your energy levels. It can cause you to overeat and take in more junk food as a way to sooth your agitation.

Unfortunately, this will lead to you having an improper balance in regards to your physiological needs. You will be unable to fulfill your motivational goals when you treat your body in this unhealthy manner.

When you are dealing with constant stress, it will also cause a number of reactions in your body. Stress can cause your muscles to tense up without you knowing it and can lead to the improper digestion of your meals and sore aching muscles.

With constant stress, you'll find it difficult to move forward in achieving your goals because you will always be having to address your health issues. Your body needs to be in good working order; otherwise, it will do nothing more than distract you from getting energized and finding the motivation to reach your goals.

If stress has taken hold of you, you might find that you are overly pessimistic which can develop a loss of interest in the things that you once loved to do. When you are looking at the world from a cynical point of view, you won't be able to find your motivation or become energized to reach your goals, leading you to become disappointed in your life.

The following suggestions are techniques that you can utilize daily to help calm yourself and reduce your stress levels.

Meditation

Meditating on a regular basis is a great way to calm your mind

and relieve stress. Your meditation practice doesn't have to take hours, but you can start to see immediate relief in your stress levels with just ten minutes of meditation a day. To begin your meditation practice, find a comfortable place to sit. Make sure that your back is completely straight. Place your feet firmly on the floor.

Now think about something that is positive, like "I can do this," or

"I will succeed in reaching my goal." Breath evenly as you think these thoughts. Continue to observe your breathing for at least ten minutes. Doing this will affect your neural pathways and will help you to work through current and future stressors.

Breathe Deeply

Every couple of hours take a 5-minute break and focus on your breathing. Sit up straight, close your eyes, and place your hand on your belly. Slowly inhale through your nose and feel the breath begin in your abdomen and work its way up to the top of your head.

Reverse the process as you exhale through your mouth. Breathing deeply in this manner helps to counter the effects of stress by slowing down your heart rate and lowering your blood pressure.

Be Present

With today's 24/7 connected world, we tend to forget that we should slow down and just be present at the moment. Take five minutes to focus on only one behavior with awareness. When you are out for a walk, notice how the air feels on your face and how your feet feel when they hit the ground.

Learn to enjoy the texture and taste of each bite of food. When you can slow down and spend time at the moment and focus on your senses, you will start to feel less tense.

Reach Out

One of your best tools for handling stress is your social network. Get out and talk to others and share with them what is going on in your life. This can give you a fresh perspective while helping to keep your connections strong.

Tune Into Your Body

Take some time every day to mentally scan your body to get a sense of how your chronic stress is affecting it every day. Lie on your back with your feet planted firmly on the floor. Start with your toes and work your way up to your scalp, and notice how your body feels.

You want just to be aware of the places throughout your body that feel tight or loose without trying to change anything. For one to two minutes, imagine each breath flowing to that part of the body. Repeat this process as you move your focus up your body, paying close attention to the sensations that you feel.

Decompress

Place a warm heat wrap around your neck and shoulders for ten minutes. Close your eyes and relax your neck, face, upper chest, and back muscles. Remove the wrap and use a tennis ball or foam roller to massage the tension away.

Laugh Out Loud

Having a good belly laugh doesn't just lighten the load mentally, but it also lowers cortisol, your body's stress hormone, and boosts chemicals in your brains called endorphins, which help your mood. Lighten things up by tuning into your favorite sitcom or video, reading comics, or talking with friends who make you smile.

Turn on the Music

Research has proven that listening to soothing music can help to lower your heart rate, lower blood pressure, and contribute to reducing anxiety. Take some time to create a playlist of your favorite songs or nature sounds and allow your mind to focus on the different instruments, melodies, and singers in the piece.

Get Moving

As mentioned in the previous chapter, getting regular physical exercise will help to boost your energy and increase your motivation. Physical activity will also help to reduce any stress that you may be experiencing. All forms of exercise can help to ease depression and anxiety by helping the brain release the feelgood chemicals and give your body a chance to practice dealing with stress.

Be Grateful

To help you remember everything good in your life, keep a gratitude journal. Being grateful for what you have in your life will help to cancel out the negative thoughts and worries that you might be experiencing. Use your journal to savor the good experiences that you encounter daily.

Don't forget to celebrate your accomplishments like mastering a new hobby or a new task at work. When you start to feel stressed, spend a few moments looking through your journal to remind yourself what really matters.

Stress and a lack of energy can be the biggest obstacles to finding your motivation and achieving success. If you can incorporate at least one of these stress-busting activities daily, you will be well on your way to eliminating the stress that is keeping you from finding your motivation and finally achieving success.

Conclusion

There are so many things in life that can quickly kill your motivation, making it hard for you to accomplish your goals and get everything in life that you desire. The tips and suggestions throughout this book are meant as a way to help you boost your energy and jump-start your motivation.

As you read through this book, you need to develop a game plan that is going to work for you. This will include altering your daily diet and choosing healthier foods and improving your physical activity and mental health.

By creating a better life, both mentally and physically, as well as emotionally, you will be more likely to succeed in achieving your goals.

With your new found motivation, you will be more likely to stay on your path to accomplishing your goals and achieving the success you deserve. The critical thing to remember is to start small and make a commitment to improving your motivation.

THE SUCCESS

www.ingramcontent.com/pod-product-compliance
Lightning Source LLC
Chambersburg PA
CBHW071348130726
47996CB00002B/845